I0486700

NO EXCUSE! in business

written by

Zsolt Szemerszky

NO EXCUSE! in business
- *written by Zsolt Szemerszky* -

First Printing: 2013

ISBN-13: 978-1519168238

ISBN-10: 1519168233

CreateSpace Independent Publishing Platform
Amazon.com

www.zsoltszemerszky.com

NO EXCUSE! in business
- *written by Zsolt Szemerszky* -

NO EXCUSE! in business
- *written by Zsolt Szemerszky* -

Contents

NO EXCUSE! in business
- written by Zsolt Szemerszky -

Introduction

Zsolt Szemerszky is a National Quality Prize Winner Revenue Specialist and Author.

His aim to help people and corporations to achieve their highest ambitions.

Being an author of multiple books, published in over 50 countries world-wide helped Zsolt Szemerszky to create business values for people and to motivate them in the road towards their aims.

One of Zsolt's most quoted sentence is:

"Every mountain can be climbed
just you have to find the appropriate way to it.
If somebody does not achieve it's goal
then he has not done everything to achieve it.
The secret of success is persistence!"

As one of the top business crisis advisor, revenue specialist, performance and marketing expert, Zsolt's books, videos, newsletters and appearances now inspire millions of people worldwide.

NO EXCUSE! in business
- written by Zsolt Szemerszky -

NO EXCUSE! in business

written by

Zsolt Szemerszky

NO EXCUSE! in business
- *written by Zsolt Szemerszky* -

Chapter 01
Everything begins from stress

It was only 18:45. I was early again, but it was perfectly fine for me. I always preferred to arrive a few minutes earlier to collect my thoughts and to get some inspiration from the atmosphere.

My dinner with John who is a very kind partner of mine was set up already two months before. He is the typical entrepreneur type of person who has built up his own company more than twenty years ago. I know him since many years. I used to consult a lot of companies from the small and medium businesses sector and I always enjoyed John's business. We have a very similar taste for whisky and cigars and I was sure that today would be a great night, when we can enjoy two big fat cuban ambassadors after our dinner.

I barely sat down when John appeared in the main door of the restaurant. He was a very tall man, with a height of almost two meters and he always wore the nicest suits I have ever seen. John always stated that we have to dress up for our businesses. I never liked to wear a tie, however I have to admit he has right. There are a lot of people who believe in casual dress, which is the new trend however based on my own experience, clients still respect you more if you dress up as a professional because you are the mirror of your company. So for John it was a badge of honor to wear his custom tailored suits, which gave him the feeling of the "power of influence" on people.

When he noticed me he welcomed me well in advance.

- Hello Zsolt - he shouted towards me from two tables distance - How are you?

I stood up and replied to him:

- Very well John, very well. I am glad you are here. How are you?

- I am fine, fine.

- Please have a seat. - I invited him to the table.

As we sat down I noticed that he is not in the perfect state. I saw that he is sweating and his veins are swollen in his forehead. He was really glowing from the stress.

- Is everything fine in business? - I asked him.

- Just the usual...

- Usually good?

From the way how he looked at me at this point I immediately knew that I made a big mistake. I opened the pipe for complains.

Few years ago I noticed that in the modern society it is usual to complain. I searched a lot for the reason and the source why we are not satisfied with our life. Finally I realized it. After I discovered the source of complaining my personal and business life started to improve. I got the chance to develop myself. It was really incredible because I realized that complaining is one of the very first thing what we learn as infants.

It is incredible how many business and life-coaching trainings are available, such as courses about improving your efficiency, your business performance, or lectures about how you can be more balanced and happier in your personal life. This is why it was really strange that we can not really read about the source of complaining. Somehow people do not really talk about this. However complaining is all around us and I believe that the key to be happier is to understand every little step of the road, which leads us towards our happiness.

Believe it or not complaining was among the very first things we have learnt as infants. This was a very easy method, which kept us alive.

People usually do things with reasons. Therefore you can also always find a reason why we are where we are in our business and/or our personal aims. Life is a big learning cycle where we all have the possibility to learn and to improve our skills. However as infants we made a huge mistake in our life. We misinterpreted some of the gestures, which started to influence our whole life.

As infants we learnt fast that if we are hungry then the only thing to do is to cry and our mother will run to us and feed us. We easily drew a lesson that crying equals with food. It was a very easy and clear message for us.

However we also learnt that when we are in pain, we can also use crying as a tool and our mother will run again to us, pick us up in her caring and loving arms to rock us to sleep. Now this was a perfectly new thing, which meant that crying equals with care and love.

Our infantile brain put the picture together very fast and the result was simple: crying equals with love, care, food. Therefore crying became our Jolly Joker card. By time we noticed and understood that we are able to reach the unconditional attention of our parents simply by crying. And let's face it, this worked very well.

However what helped our survival in our very first years was a "virus", which infected our future. This was a "virus", which made us addictive and this still proliferates deep in our body.

So we mixed up the attention with love as the purpose of our own survival. But the two thing are definitely not the same. This is the reason why many of us have never experienced real, true and unconditional love. Once I heard in a conference that we are living in an "ego life". The term ego life seems to be true because many of us love other people around us for what they can do for us, and not for the fact who they really are.

So then why are we complaining?
Because we want attention!

People usually speak about their problems because they want attention. Attention, audition, understanding and absolution that everything will be fine and they did not do anything wrong. However if we agree with the Law of Attraction, namely the name given to the belief that "like attracts like" and that by focusing on positive or negative thoughts, one can bring about positive or negative results, then we can easily state that by complaining we will attract only crap around us. When we are complaining then our brain and our spirit is focusing with full energy on the negative stuff, so let's put a bet on what life will bring us...

I can clearly state that there is nothing wrong with being afraid. In every situation when something happens differently from our plans we can easily loose our faith and we can go into hesitation. Even if it is hard to acknowledge for us during those times we all have fear in our heart. We are all afraid from sudden changes, the new things and from the unknown. It is a natural human reaction. However it is not natural to focus on the problems instead of their potential solutions. When we were infants we had no other choice in our hands, but now as grownups the decision is in our hands and it is only ours.

But tonight there was no way back, I gave John the chance to complain and he took it. So I was a good friend and I started to prepare myself for an emotionally intense conversation.

Chapter 02
Discovering the source

- So how is business? - I tried to release John's thoughts.

- Well, business sucks. - he replied shortly, but for me these words were more than enough to understand that his revenue is down.

- What happened?

- The economy sucks and our sales numbers are down. - he started - We are working more and more every day, but we are gaining less and less results.

Suddenly John hang his head and I started to feel his very honest pain. I knew that I should be quiet and give him some space and time before he continues.

- Sometimes I feel that I am the only one who really cares about this. I am the only one who really works in this company.

- But you have a great product and as far as I remember your selling always went well in the last twenty years. - I tried to put John back on to the positive track, but he did not give me any chance for this. He just presented me the first excuse.

- Yes, but this time it is different and it all started a few years ago.

Oh boy, I knew that I will have to listen to the nice old presentation of the economic crisis and its effects, but I was also well prepared to handle this. Not to mention that I was hundred percent sure that at the end of the day John will stand up from our dinner with a multi-million mind solution.

- You know Zsolt, the market has changed.

I frowned but I wanted to listen to his version before I would start any argument.

- Go on, John.

- Everything started with the economic crash a few years ago. People lost huge parts of their wealth and they became very deliberate. They are watching and monitoring the market and business is not the same anymore.

- Indeed John - I tried to acknowledge him to ensure him the feeling that I am on his side.

- And then the Internet!

- What Internet? - My eyebrows went very high at this point because the Internet is way more older than the last economic crisis.

- You know, all the cheap products on the Internet. - said John in a very angry tone. I saw that his blood temperature is going up very fast as he continued. - We have the best products and solutions but our clients are still searching for new and newer discounts. We simply can not keep them without pulling down our trousers. And that's what kills us.

This was the point where I decided to start my argument. Specially because the changes in the market can be very positive as well. I was never afraid from a little challenge and I believe that this was the point when I could motivate a little bit my old friend John.

- So let me understand your problem - I started - You have prospective clients who are interested in your products, right?

- Yes, we are presenting our portfolio in many places.

- So, you have prospective clients who are interested in your products and who need your products, right?

- Right. But we can not bring them into our umbrella because they are always looking for cheaper prices or just giving us those excuses.

- Excuses? What type of excuses? - I asked him back.

- You know, time, budget, etc... - said John in a more quiet way than before. I really felt that his mood has changed from anger into a depressed one. - And frankly, I can understand them. This current economy sucks.

At this point I could not stand not to smile. However John did not share my happiness and he immediately asked me point-blank:

- Why the hell on Earth are you smiling?

- Let's play a role game and I will tell you.

- I am not in the mood to play.

I started to feel that he deserves some explanation.

- Okay John. Look, you have good products and you have prospective clients. However one of your major problem is that your sympathy does not allow you to close those deals.

- It is not true!

- Then play with me.

- Okay.

What I really wanted to make John understand was that ninety percent of the lost sales come from the excuses not handled.

- Perfect. Let's say that you are my prospective buyer. - I started.

- Okay.

- And please drop me some of the excuses you hear day by day. I promise you I will not allow you to leave the restaurant without a sales contract.

John finally smiled and I started to see the expression in his face that he will catch me now. He was perfectly sure that he can drop me an excuse that I can not handle. I allowed him in this belief and I started...

- So, let's say that you listened to my presentation of the my product that I want to sell to you. You had some interesting questions on its technical details, but you do not want to buy it yet. Drop me your excuses why you do not want to buy it.

- Thank you for this presentation, but I do not need this. - smiled John.

- If you would not need the product I offer here then we would not sit here today.

- Yes, but it is expensive.

- Yes, it is expensive. - I replied to John, who started to feel some kind of satisfaction.

I gave him the moment to enjoy this almost winning feeling then I continued.

- Yes, it is expensive because it brings you the requested result. Every thing that brings you result can not be considered expensive. The only thing that you can call expensive are those things that do not bring you any result. I am hundred percent sure that you are a man who is looking for a result oriented solution instead of a cheap one.

John started to be a little bit uncomfortable, but we both knew that it is very early to give it up.

- Okay, but we do not have this amount planned in our budget. - John showed his evil smile to me.

- I understand this. As I see you are looking for a solution to improve your business performance. Since we are talking about price you already understood that our product brings you results.

- Yes, but... - and here I cut immediately into the words of John.

- So yes, the result is a key question for you. We can agree on this. With proper results you can increase your income and revenue so the only question is when would you like to gain more profit?

- Okay, but I need to talk with the headquarter.

- I am pretty sure that the headquarter and your bosses are aiming at the same thing, to gain more profit. Do you believe they do not want improvement?

- Of course they want it, but I need to see other solutions as well to compare them.

- You are entitled to do it. However you just mentioned that you are looking at the result instead of the price. I am sure that you are looking for the best product for your company and I am very confident that if we sign a contract you will be very satisfied at the end of the day.

John reclined and he pined me his question with a smile on his face.

- You do not let me out from this, right?

- No. Because you have the intent to buy, you have the money to own my product and the only thing missing is your confident that you want to sign the contract with me now.

- So it is all about excuses? - asked John.

- In ninety percent of the cases, yes.

- That's a lot.

- What is really a lot my fried is the margin you loose by not handling these excuses and letting your prospective clients to go to your competitors. This is why most of the companies are struggling because they are letting the prospective client to make new runs with other competitors.

- It is probably true. - said John.

- And believe it or not if you have targeted well your prospective client then he has money and intent so the only question is wether he buys it directly from you or from your competitors.

I saw on John's face that he is thinking very hard. I almost heard the cogwheels ticking inside his head. I saw that he really wants to ask something, but I felt that my strong character friend became very shy at this point. Then he composed his thoughts together and I received his big question.

- Do you think this is working in the crisis as well?

- John, come on, we are not in a crisis.

- Yes, but we live it's after effects.

I was not really sure why, but I decided to give him some explanation regarding my point of views. I decided to show him how he can grow in crisis, how he can close much more prospective clients. But I wanted to clear his mind first, I wanted to release his thoughts and implement positive ones instead of the negative ones.

Luckily I got a breathing space because our waiter finally arrived.

Chapter 03
Entrepreneur or Leader

- Do you know what the difference is between an entrepreneur and a leader? - I asked John.

- Of course. An entrepreneur owns his own business while a leader works in a high position in one of my companies. - he laughed at me loudly.

- So, you have good leaders, right? - I winked at John.

- Yes, the best ones. - he smiled with satisfaction on his face.

- And is it necessary for an entrepreneur to be a leader?

- Yes, of course. - John answered promptly.

- So the leader is a higher status, right?

I saw on John's face that he disagrees with me, but he also hesitated to answer because he knew that I will prove him wrong.

- I always create a bold line between an entrepreneur and a leader. - I started to explain to John my philosophy - I believe that not all entrepreneurs are designed to survive. I think the economic crisis clearly presented how easy it is to lose our businesses and fortunes, and I believe one of the reason why companies went bankrupt is because their leaders had no real life experience to survive.

- How the hell is this related to my business? If you state that I will go down then I am out of here. - said John with anger as well as fear in his voice.

- No, no. Please do not misunderstand me. - I tried to calm him down.

I know from all my experiences that we all have fears when someone holds a mirror in front of us showing us our mistakes. And many of us feel that these are attacks and punches into our face. However presenting mistakes and giving additional ways to correct them is a great chance to improve our skills. I continued the chain of my thoughts.

- When I started my first company I was very motivated with it. It was my tool to gain whatever I want in my life. I worked ten-twelve hours per day in the beginning and I really enjoyed it. Not to mention that as you know success came very soon. After three years I had my dream cars, a Range Rover and a Lotus and I really felt that I am alive. I am sure you know as well how it feels to sign the first big contract, to receive the first million in your bank account or to be handled as a respected solution provider and a respected business owner in your community.

John sat there, his eyes twinkled like bright stars on the night sky. He clearly knew what this feeling was like.

- In those time I had a "lifestyle" business.

- "Lifestyle" business? But you are a revenue specialist and business process optimizer? - asked John with huge surprise in his voice.

- Yes, "lifestyle" business because for me the definition of "lifestyle" business is when you are working hard, gaining the results that you want and providing a good environment for yourself. You get almost everything you want. Ergo you are able to create a nice lifestyle for yourself.

- Ok, I understand what you mean.

- So this worked well in the first five years and I have to tell you that in those times I really enjoyed it. Then suddenly I realized that I am still working twelve hours every day in my office, sometimes even more. I also realized that my stress level has increased. I felt that I am working much more for the company than any other paid employee.

- I know this feeling. - smiled John.

- Yes, but this led me to the point that I hardly even saw my wife and I started to know my family only from pictures.

I stopped here for a moment because I felt that I needed to drink a little bit of water. My mouth started to dry out because as I was talking, I went through these periods emotionally again in my head.

- Many people said that successful people work more, but in my opinion this is bullshit. Successful people know something better, which I never did well before, but I am doing it now day by day.

- What? - inquired John very intensively.

- The art of delegation.

- But we all delegate in our business...

- But how? Are you satisfied with its results? - I asked him back.

And boom! John was shocked, because he immediately understood that without the adequate results there should be some problem. A problem for which he is also responsible.

- You know in the old times the man worked hard, he sent the money home and the family was happy. I think it is acceptable, specially when you have a very young child. However I wanted to be happy too. I wanted to gain things that I can enjoy too.

- And your family?

- Look, when you work hard, your family enjoys the result, however when you feel tired and overloaded then something is clearly wrong. I think when you work hard, your family is happy and if you are happy too then your life is on the right track. Working for others without enjoying your life is slavery. It does not help your life.

John nodded his head very intensively. He knew that I know that we works his ass out for his family and sometimes he can not go home before midnight.

- So I realized that I gave up my lifestyle business and I converted myself into an entrepreneur. Which by definition an entrepreneur is someone who is fighting with his competitors for his own survival. And this is where his challenges of life has been converted into daily problems, has increased his stress level and the endless business hours. In the meantime he is fighting for new income sources while he knows his family only by photos. All this causes a lot of stress and in most cases an early burn out.

- You are speaking from my heart. - said John and he asked for another drink from the waiter.

- Yeah, but I did not start business for this. I never wanted to fight for my own survival.

- None of us did...

Where are our drinks? Where are our drinks? Probably this was on John's mind, because he was involved in this entrepreneur feeling very deeply.

- On the other hand if I would describe a real visionary or a leader I would say they are very happy people with a lot of free time. They are able to focus on their hobbies as well, while they are earning incredible amounts of money and of course they can spend valuable time with their family.

That is what I want. - John agreed with me promptly.

- What I realized John, is that successful people are able to delegate the biggest part of the tasks. They are able to approach people who are ready to help them to realize their aims. And this is when you will become a real leader and/or a business owner.

- True.

- Because you as an owner you have the vision for your company. You had the guts to start to accomplish your aim. Therefore you have to lead your employees and you have to ensure them your knowledge and guidance to get the jobs done. You know all successful people are enjoying their businesses, they are happy because they are able to focus on their own aims and visions. And this is the key, to develop a team who is ready to make your delegated visions come true.

- Do you think it is easy? Where the hell are these super human employees grow? - asked John sarcastically.

- Well my friend, they are growing in your garden. Because it is all upon you. No one will find out your thoughts. You have to be there to let them know the right way and to guide them to the how.

Big silence covered us, which was the silence of realization. I wanted to break this silence fast before it turned into lethargy.

- Look let me draw you something related to problems.

So I picked up one of the tea-cloth, I got my pen out and I started to draw for John.

Chapter 04
The problems distract your focus

First of all I drew for John a line, which represented the past, the present and the future. The left end was the past, the right end was the future and I placed a human figure into the middle where the present was. I placed a "goals" sign on the right side and my little figure faced directly the sign.

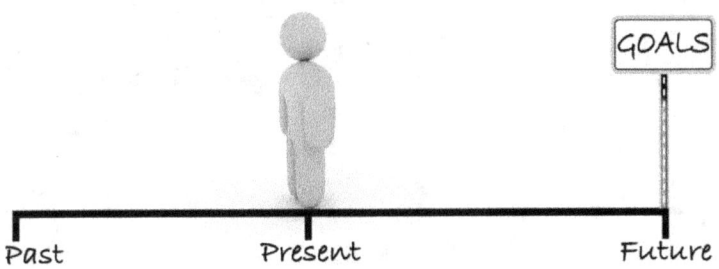

- This is you, my friend. - I said to John.

- I like that I am thin but I am not bold. - he joked back.

- You are right but believe me you do not want hair in this picture.

- Why?

- Because the hair, or let's say the lines of your hair represent your problems. But let me explain it to you.

- I am really curious. - laughed John, who had no idea what I am talking about.

- Okay. So in a perfect state our guy is watching forward towards his aims. As you can see his eyes are focusing without any distraction. This is what all the leaders and visionaries are aiming to do. Because if you are able to get a clear view on your goals then you have a much better chance to approach them. However the reality is very different, specially nowadays.

I continued my drawing and I started to draw the margins for the field of success or let's say I was ready to outline the border of the survival of his business venture.

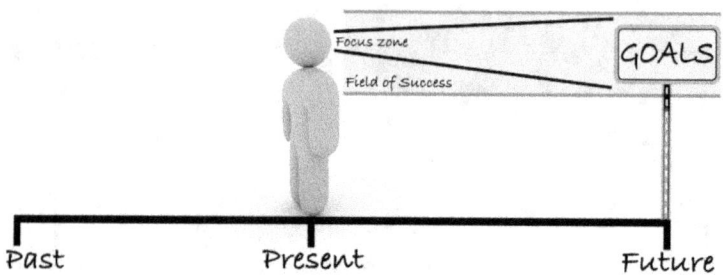

Past   Present   Future

- So this is the border, which separates success from the insecurity and failures. Until your focus is in this field you can reach any aim. However problems are always distracting you.

- Usually.

- Yes, but if you can delegate and solve your problems, your focus comes back to your goal. However unsolved problems can easily remove your attention because they will pull your focus back to the past.

I started to draw him the unsolved problems and all of these problems were connected with a line to the head of our figure. This represented his hair. What really was different now in the figure was the angle of the eyes.

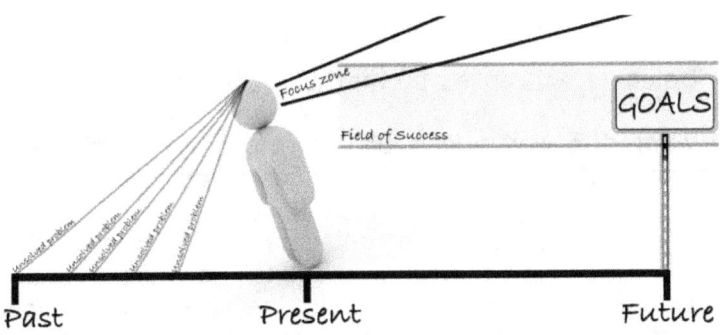

- As you can see all the "lines" represent unsolved problems.

- Got it.

- The source of the unsolved problems is coming from the past. It is like a rule, because if you could not solve and close a problem, then you probably did not handle its source. And even if you can not really see their effects believe me that they will pull you back and slow you down in the future.

- I have some of these. But do you know what I miss?

- What? - I asked John.

- Time to handle them.

- Success is coming with solved problems and released mind my friend. As you can see all the problems are related to the head of our "little John". And these little lines are pulling back his attention. This means he will loose his focus from his goals and instead he will start to focus on the unsolved problems.

- Yeah, but he has to solve the problems, right?

- No. A leader, a company owner or a visionary can not work on daily problems, otherwise his company will never develop towards the settled goals.

- So what do they do, just sit and watch?

- Delegate. - I replied promptly.

I wanted to wait a little bit more to give him the time to digest the information then I continued.

- A real leader is able to delegate the daily tasks and he is capable to control the results. However a leader needs to focus on the results because this is how improvement comes. A company owner becomes an entrepreneur when he loses his focus on the development and future aims. Just imagine how daily problems and stress distracts your positive thinking. This is why you have to convert yourself to be a good leader.

- I can do that.

- Of course you can do that!

I felt that John started to realize the power of this small drawing and he understood well that his eyes look far away from the target. He also understood that if he is the one who solves everything in his company he will never look forward towards his goals, only backwards to the problems. He had a clear vision at this point to have a delegation method in action. John was ready and motivated to convert himself into a leader. I know it is a long process, but I was happy to see his determination.

- Do you remember my very first book?

- The Inspirationaliste?

- No, the Creating Business Value.

- Yes, yes. The small guideline.

- Yes. - I smiled at John - And do you remember the first chapter "The angle of incidence of the Sun"?

- Yes, stating that everything depends on me, right?

- Right. And also that the decision to improve is in your hands. "Economy, politics, weather, your neighbor, etc... it is easy to blame these factors for your failure, but believe it or not these factors influence also your competition not only you." - I quoted the book - So put back your focus John.

I was very happy at this point because John started to be more relaxed. In the first moments when he arrived to our dinner he was very frustrated and he really needed some fresh thoughts. So I decided to cheer him up and give him some more ideas.

- Do you know the joke about the Chinese girl?

- No.

- Two girls with long hair are meeting in an event. The browned hair girl wears her hair loose on her shoulders. The black haired girl wears her hair in a ponytail. This girl has almond shaped eyes so the other girl asks her:

- Are you from China?

- No, it is just my ponytail, which is way too tight.

- Idiot. - laughed John. - But I got the message. I do not want to look like a Chinese boy just because of my problems. So let's make sail and let's go forward! - he said with a little toast for me.

We lifted our glasses and finally we enjoyed something more than simple water. Finally I could taste my favorite eighteen years old Chivas Regal.

Chapter 05
The angle of incidence of the Sun

One of the most basic and important business rule is that you are responsible for all your decisions, success or failures. Only you!

However hard it is you can not blame the external factors. We are in the same business jungle and the rules are the same for all of us. No exceptions. It is all upon you if you will survive or not. It is all upon you if you will be a Rabbit or you will become a Tiger. Now days the business is your jungle, your playground.

If you do not like to be a Rabbit then change it. You are the master of your destiny. Do not blame others, that's the game of losers and cowards.

Never blame outside factors, never say what could be if... You need to focus only on what you can do now with all your assets. You need to bring out the best as much as possible from your current, existing knowledge, assets.

Economy, politics, weather, your neighbor, etc... it is easy to blame these factors for your failure, but believe it or not these factors influence also your competition not only you.

You can not change these factors, just as you can not change the politics. You need to accept them, acknowledge the rules and go forward towards your aims. Sitting and waiting for the changes is equal with suicide because you will lose the control over things.

Chapter 06
Crisis = Potential

Many minutes passed by silently between me and John and I started to watch his emotions. I felt that he is in trouble and he has something, which will come out soon. I was perfectly sure that he understands that handling the excuses is among the most important key issues in business, but there is much more to do. I was also aware that people who are out of their business stability are way more careful to change.

Based on many years of experience I decided to wait until he comes up with the things, which are really bothering him. Fortunately he was very fast.

- There is one thing which bugs me - he started.

- Tell me. Let's hear it.

- We are in a crisis. - he looked at me, then he continued soon. - Okay, we are in the after effect of the crisis, but my clients still feel it.

- You know in China the word "crisis" is written with two symbols.

- I did not know that. Is it relevant? - asked John.

- Yes. - I replied quickly. - The first symbol means "crucial" and the second symbol means "opportunity". So in China the word crisis contains the "crucial" or the "opportunity" symbol as well.

- Okay, I know it, the decision is mine. The angle of incidence of the Sun, right. - John started very sarcastically - However it is not easy. The crisis is usually crucial.

- The decision is always yours! - I replied to him in a little bit louder way, I wanted him to realize that he is dropping an excuse on me regarding non-performance.

The one thing what I really hated in business is non-performance. Many people are lazy to do their homework or are simply just not ready to look around and to challenge their situations. However I have to admit that more than thirteen years ago I was the same too. I started to gain knowledge from the books, but when something happened which was not written in the books I started to panic.

After many years life crossed my roads with Dodo Newman, the Inspirationaliste and she taught me one very important thing, which was to not give up our beliefs in a positive solution. She taught me to keep up and to continuously believe in my aims. Most of us are ready to give up the fight without even realizing that maybe we are already in the finish line. Thanks to Dodo I realized that I can always challenge the existing because we are able to improve things, to innovate. Since then I also know and this became my philosophy, that if you try something you never lose, however you immediately lose when you give it up. So I was ready to pick up my pen again and to draw a new thing for John.

- You can do the same old methods hoping to survive or you can take the opportunity and challenge your market. - I started.

- It is easy to say.

- No, it is not. What is easy is to wait. - I replied back to John - Have you ever read books from Dr. Spencer Johnson?

- Spencer who? - John asked back.

- Dr. Spencer Johnson. He wrote a great book called "Who moved my cheese?".

- What? - John had no idea what I meant.

- It is a book about four little mice. They are all looking for the cheese in a maze in a very changing and challenging time. The cheese represents their survival, cheese being a metaphor for what we want to have in life. - I smiled back to John.

- I am in a maze too. Ha-ha.

- You have to read the book because it is one of my favorite and it 's message is perfectly clear about one thing, the why and the when you should start to change.

- And does it help in crisis?

- Yes, because crisis could be your biggest potential my friend!

John started to see me as a very weird creature because he continuously measured my face and emotions. So I turned the other side of the tea-cloth and I started to draw on it a new picture for him. I created five buildings for John. All the buildings were different in size and width.

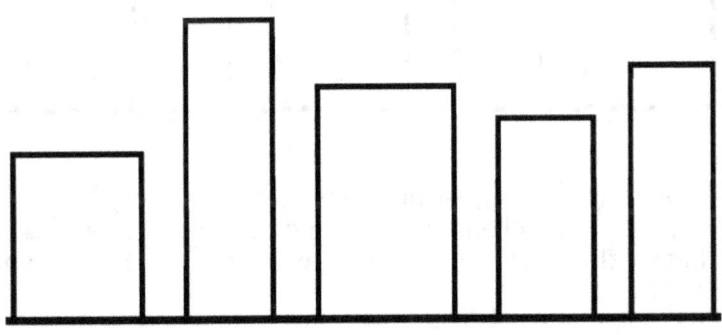

- New York? I was there! - John said.

- Nope. It is another place were you are now. - I winked with my eyes at John. - It is your business and your competitors.

- I wish I would have only four competitors. - he laughed.

- Four is good enough for today.

- Go on. - he gave me the sign that he is ready to listen to what I am aiming to tell him.

- Most of the companies are fighting for new clients during ideal business climates. There are always new clients no matter how is the economic climate is. There are not so many new clients during bad economic periods but you can still always find some.

So I drew a few "NC" combination of letters around the buildings, standing for the New Clients.

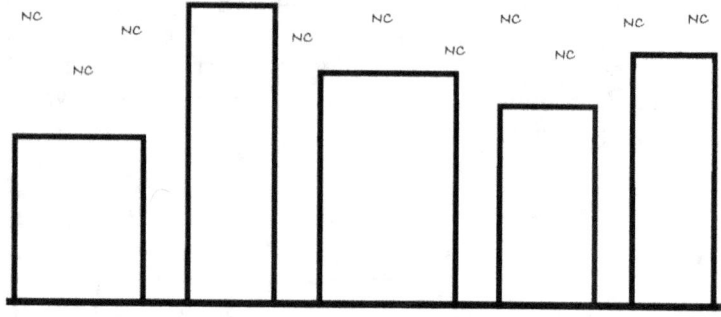

- However the biggest problem is that it is very hard to target the new clients in changing economic situations. That's it! Finally you agree with me. - John said happily.

- Wait my friend, just wait. - I calmed him down, however by now John sat back on his chair and he seemed extremely satisfied.

- Go on, go on.

- So when the economic situation is changing, let's say you are facing an after effect of a crisis, corporates start to cut back their marketing budget. They are doing this because they realize the truth that targeting those new clients is becoming very tricky and often ineffective. Therefore budget cutting makes sense for them.

- Yes. This is what I am doing too. - John agreed with me.

- Yes, but this is why you are struggling.

- Or surviving.

- John, my friend, you are hoping to survive just as all the companies who are following this strategy. However relying only on hope makes a very weak chance for you. Let me tell you why.

- I am sitting here with open ears.

- Okay. When companies are cutting back their marketing budget they act according to the Law of attraction. They will start to loose clients.

- No, they loose clients because of the crisis.

- If you want you can see it from this point of view, but that means you are influenced by the crisis and you are just going with the flow.

I saw on John's face that he wants to disagree but I gave him no time for this so I continued immediately.

- Let's put it in this way. In crisis you are loosing clients, which forces your company to cut back the budget to avoid further instability. Is this right?

- Right. I like it this way.

- Okay. The problem with instability is that your whole environment feels it. Not to mention that companies who lost clients between fifteen or twenty percent can be very insecure or even they can go bankrupt. And what does this mean?

I started to extend my draw again and John listened and watched very carefully. So I drew the twenty percent margin lines. I also drew the "LC" signs, which stood for the Lost Clients and under the margin line I drew the "C" signs, which represented the Clients.

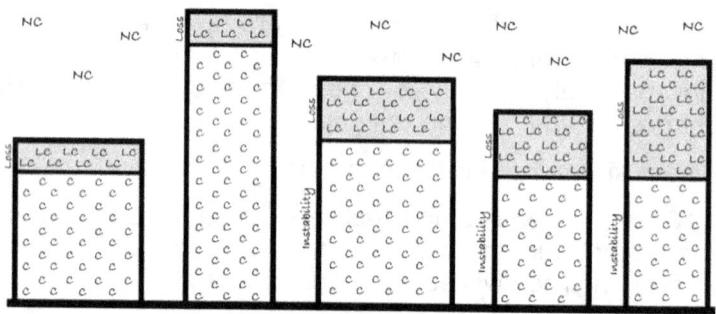

- Okay. These are the twenty percent lines where the instability starts. Of course this can be more or less depending on the size and the reserve of the company.

- Got it.

- As you can see there are plenty of Lost Clients in the twenty percent margin. We usually never target them, because it requires too much effort to get them under our umbrella. Not to mention that many of the lost clients have no more funds to restart properly or even if they have they will cause much more extra work.

- Why? They are free clients on the market.

- No they are lost clients on the market.

- Without supplier.

- Without trust and probably without the necessary amount to restart. Trust me they need much more effort and investments.

- So what would you do? - John asked.

- I would target the Clients who stayed, the "C"-s.

I saw on John's face that he is very surprised and I started to feel that he is looking at me as a fool. So I drew a little "P" letter in front of all the "C"-s so we get the combination of letters "PC", which represent now the Prospective Clients.

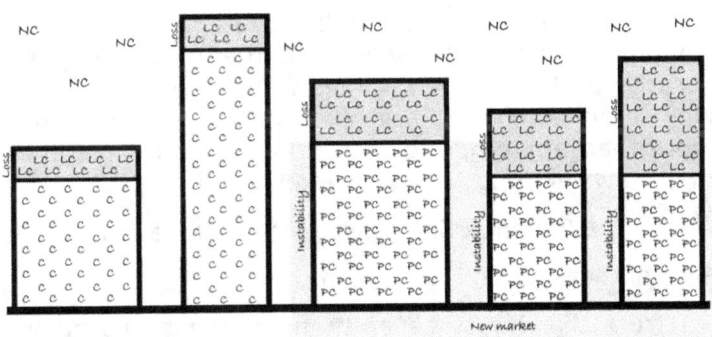

- Look, in crisis people are looking for different values than before. Price and marketing blah-blah are becoming a lower priority. In these times the clients are looking for stability, trust and long term solutions. Therefore the market needs are changing.

- Indeed.

- So if you target your new clients in the same old way, you will realize that you are doing the same old strategy and you will receive much less result. And this is your fault because you let yourself being effected by the outside factors without thinking outside the box and challenging the existing potentials.

- So you would target the competitors?

- Yes. I would target all the clients who already invested into your competitors. I would offer them the same product for the same price or even higher.

- Higher? Then why the hell would they change to us for a higher price?

- Because in crisis clients seek stability in the first place. Price becomes the third or much lower priority. If you are able to offer stability, security and you can gain their trust then you have a whole new market. And believe it or not they will be happy to change companies if you can convince them regarding the security and the added values from your side. This is why smart companies are able to grow even ten times more than any others during troubled economic times. Crisis always brings a new market.

- Says the Revenue Specialist. - John started to laugh.

- I feel that you do not trust in this.

- I trust this I just never thought about this before. Especially not from this point of view.

- Thinking outside the box my friend. Thinking outside the box. You know amateurs are trying to push and force their corporate messages meanwhile professionals are realizing the market gap, selecting the prospective clients and targeting them. If you are going with the average you will receive the same result than the average. However if you are ready to challenge the existing economic situations then you have the possibility to grow.

- I agree. - John acknowledged.

- Then you can also agree with my previous thought that in crisis you never cut back your marketing budget because it is your tool to communicate with the prospective clients. You just reorganize your focus and you definitely send out the message that you are not effected by the crisis, you are there and your stability is hard as a rock.

- It is definitely a new perspective. Thanks.

- You are welcome.

I saw that John is very satisfied and he is already thinking about his next steps tomorrow. But I knew him very well so I could not stand to ask him what else bothers him.

Chapter 07
Price fight

- What else?

- What-what else? - John asked me back.

- What else bugs you?

- Nothing but the strategy. The right way.

- You mean by...?

- The price. The price of course - said John finally.

I remained quiet because I was sure about this from the very beginning. Unfortunately business people have a kind of automatism that the easiest way to win a business is by giving discounts. However I think this is the laziest and the less effective way. Less effective because sales guys easily give discounts, which reduce and kill our profits. Engineers are ready to provide extra services, which is increased work not compensated by the client. Therefore I would never consider the decreased pricing as a marketing or a sales tool. It is simply not healthy for the business.

- Look John, there are three very different issues here. The first one is the crisis, which is one of the greatest tool to improve your income. However we can also talk about the competitor fight and the price fight, which are two very different issues. To handle the competitors and the price issue you have to make a difference.

- Yes, but we are in the same field.

- And then what? Is it a problem?

- Ok, what about the price? - asked John.

- Please do not avoid my question. Let me explain it in a very short way.

- Okay.

- The main problem is what you have also probably noticed that the number of the newly formed companies are intensively growing. All of them are looking for profit, however they can not offer the same price levels as their competitors, which are already in the market since twenty plus years. So ninety-nine percent of the newbies are playing the same old card, which is: they are cheaper.

- That's it! - said John with a huge acceptance in his voice.

- But this is the trap. They can not provide high quality on low price however as it seems the high quality service providers are forced to reduce their prices. Therefore if you are joining this game you will loose your profit.

- What can I do?

- You can make a difference by realizing something.

- What? What? - asked John in a very excited way. He was like a child in the chocolate store. He wanted the answer immediately.

- That something is relative. None of the products or solutions have an absolute value. How much is the value of a product? Exactly the same what your customer is ready to pay for it.

- Yeah, but everybody wants the cheapest solution.

- Really?

- Really.

- Did you buy the cheapest suit?

- No. Of course not.

- Did you buy the cheapest car?

- No.

- Are we eating now in the cheapest restaurant?

- No.

- So does the price really matter?

- In these cases no.

- The price never really matters! When you are able to provide something that the client wants and what makes a real difference in your market, then the price becomes a secondary issue. The real problem is that most of the marketing people can not educate the prospective clients.

- What do you mean by this? - asked back John.

- The price. This is what all the customers see. Why?

- Because it is obvious?

- Because there is nothing else. A good marketing strategy is capable to educate the client to the benefits, related services, added values and it shows the prospective clients why is it makes a positive difference to buy that specific product or solution from you.

- Client education.

- Yes and with client education you are able to form your market or even more you are able to open a new market for yourself. Even if you sell the same product as your competitors you still have the possibility to make a difference.

- So it is all about the additional things?

- John, why the hell are you going to a restaurant?

- I do not know. Really. - he laughed.

- I am not going to the restaurant because of the food, because I can cook too. I am pretty sure that when you are hungry you can make something nice at home. I am not going there either to meet with my friends or business partners, because I can meet with them anywhere else.

- So why are we here?

- Because of the service. - I stopped for a little moment then I continued. - The service is what really counts. I am coming here because I like how they are seating me, how they are serving me and not to mention that for these hours they give me the feeling that I get something special in exchange for my money.

- Added value.

- Difference my friend, difference. If I would only see the price tag I would cook at home. The price never really counts.

- It maybe sounds stupid but I am starting to agree with you - said John and this felt very good.

Chapter 08
The richness of our roots

Finally we were on track and John started to understand that price does not really matter if you are able to educate your target group. He was clearly aware that until this point he went into a price fight just because he missed this key factor. John realized that he followed the wrong type of marketing approach.

The real marketing approach is a process, which builds up a value for a product. This converts a potentially valuable product into a really valuable one. We both knew that if a client really wants something then price does not really matter anymore. However I continued our little conversation because I wanted to clarify this in John.

- People accept the price for sure. Because price is easy, everybody knows that 149 is less than 219.

- Yes. This is how they purchase things.

- If you allow them to compare your product based simply on price, then you can start to dig the grave for your company. - I said to John, who looked really sad.

- Yes, but... - and he did not finish his sentence, so I broke the silence.

- Look, remember why you bought your car? Was it the cheapest? And your suit?

And at this point I started to see again that sparkle in John's eyes. His mind came back to our reality and he started to remember all that we talked about a few minutes ago. Human brain usually focuses on the negative effects so we always need to remind our brain of the positive things and thoughts as well.

- If you are a smart leader then you can educate your target group. Everybody can see the price, but we have to show them our values as well. Look...

I tried to find some more space on our tea-cloth and I started to draw for John again. I drew him two trees. Both trees had the similar size of crown, but their trunks were different in size. And because of the difference of the trunk they had different types of roots as well. I also drew our little figure standing between the two trees.

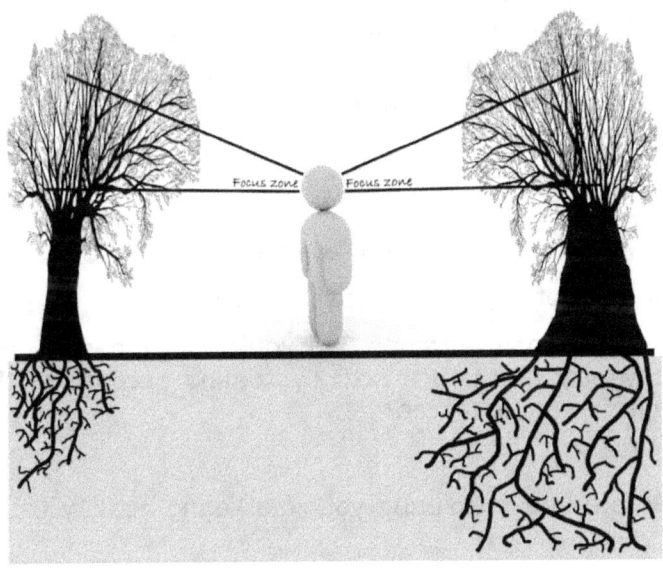

- In a calm economic situation and without being educated this is how clients see the companies. - I started.

- As a tree? - joked John.

- Yes, as a tree. A tree where everybody is looking at the tree crown, which is the biggest visible surface. Let's say it is the packaging of the tree, therefore all marketing experts are aiming to present it in the most delicate and fancy way.

- Got it. This is what makes the difference.

- If you are in the price fight, then yes. - I agreed with John. - When a prospective client sees two similar companies with two similar price tags then he will decide based on the "packaging". This is where the marketing usually focuses on.

- The amateur marketing? - John asked back curiously.

- Let's say the marketing which focuses on the brand message instead of the intense growth of new clients.

- Yes, but making beautiful advertisements and presenting them everywhere is a good result.

- Specially if you can measure it.

- I can.

- How? - I asked back immediately.

- Number of appearances per countries.

- A question my friend: Can you really measure how many new clients are actually coming because of the magazine appearances?

- Not really.

- So are you measuring your marketing activity based on weight?

- What? - asked John with some confusion in his voice.

- Yes, based on kilogram. Because when you spend 1 million for media appearances and you receive 100 magazines but not measurable results, then you are paying for the weight of the media appearances instead of the number of the new clients.

- But...

- Look, the situation is that unmeasurable marketing tools are always a waste of money.

- Media appearance is a waste of money?

- No. Media appearance is good if you can measure their results. Measuring is critical because it gives you back feed-back and feed-backs help your business to react in a proper way to the market needs. Marketing is all about achieving reaction in order to attract the attention of your prospective clients.

- This is true. - acknowledged it John.

I started to draw again, because I did not want to go deeply into this media advertisement issue, I could talk about its benefits or its negative effects for hours. Instead of this I changed the focus of our little figure from the tree crown to the roots of the tree.

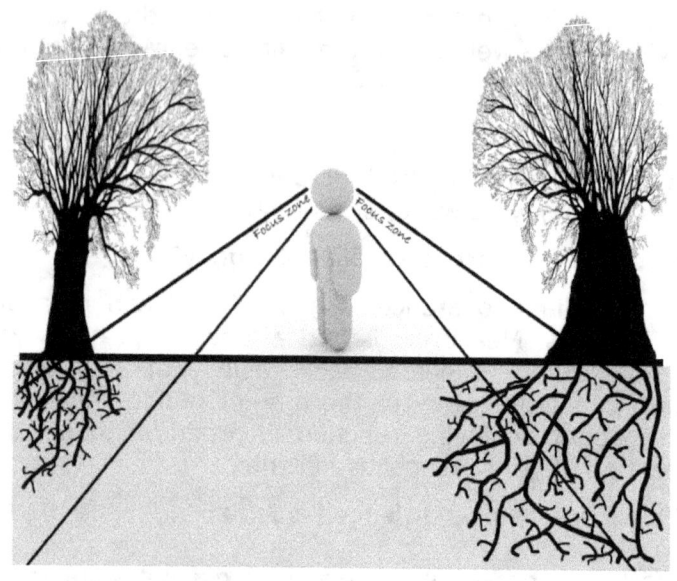

- The values are usually hidden, just as you can not see the roots of the trees. As I mentioned to you before in difficult economic situations people are looking for stability.

- Yes, targeting the competitors' clients who feel unstable. Got it. - John winked.

- Yes. - I smiled back to John. - Because when people are looking for stability their focuses are changing. They are not looking anymore at the fancy tree-bush, not even at the tree trunk, but at the roots. Prospective clients will try to make their decision based on the roots of the tree.

- But it is hidden.

- Yes, if you are not presenting it to them.

- Under the ground?

- Is your company under the ground? - I asked back.

- No, hell no - shouted John. - We are alive!

- Then please see the tree as a symbolic drawing.

- Okay-okay. - smiled John.

- So, if you are able to present the roots, then you are able to educate your prospective clients to the added values and to the extra stability that they can reach. But at this point you have to understand one thing.

- What?

- That marketing is not about the product or the service itself.

- I am starting to be confused.

- Marketing is all about people. The thing is that in an economic climate where the supplies are much higher than the demand is, advertisement is only good for the magazines but not for the businesses itself. Marketing is all about people. - I repeated it to John.

I pointed again to the drawing, which I made a few minutes ago and I showed the focus of the figure to John.

- As you can see the roots are what really count because people are looking for values, which gives them security and stability. This is how you can make a bold difference in your market and this is how you can control it without being effected by any kind of negative economic situation. However do not forget that the market is always changing, therefore you continuously need to follow and challenge it.

- Got it.

- Then here is more. - I continued. - Every leader knows that if your company is not able to generate profit then it will not survive for a long time. But fewer leader understands that if you can not create value for your clients then you have no future.

After this sentence John became very quiet. It looked like that he is focusing only on his meal but I knew that his cogwheels are ticking deep inside his head. I also knew that I need to give him some time again to digest all he heard. These were a lot of information for him and most of them from a different point of view which he was used to. So I started to enjoy my meal as well and I was ready to answer his upcoming questions. I was sure there will be some soon, but we had time to wait because we have not finished our dinner yet, not to mention our cigar time at the end. It was our routine to enjoy them after our dinner.

Chapter 09
Loan is a chain

- What about loans - asked John from out of the blue.

- What loans? - I asked back with surprise, because I had no idea how the question of loan is related to our previous conversation.

- Let's say you have developed a new service or product, you have created a smart campaign, but you do not have enough money to start it in big. Would you take up a loan?

I knew where this conversation would go and since I had good and bad experiences with loans it was still very hard to answer John. I have a very biased opinion about loans, but it is only my point of view and I did not wanted to force it on to John. So I tried to give him the middle, diplomatic way.

- If you are hundred percent sure about your product, if you have created tons of surveys regarding its marketability, if you get back enough feed-backs whereby the prospective clients really need your product and if you trust your strategy without any hesitation, then you can take up a loan.

- There are a lot of "if"s... - laughed John.

- Yes, because loan is a kind of chain on your hands.

- Yes, you have to pay it back.

- Pay it back with an interest and you sign it in a situation where you have no basic funds, not even extra funds for the interest.

- But it will come later.

- Yes, if you have created a savvy strategy with a lot of surveys and analysis supporting it.

- Indeed.

I could not stand not to draw him again something. So I started to draw how I envision the issue of loan.

- Look, here is a scale - I said to John. - The left side is your costs and debt.

- Okay. But do not draw too much there. - John smiled.

- Just a little. - I winked him back. - And the right side is your income.

- Got it.

- We both know that when the scale is equal then we are in the level of survival.

- Yep. - agreed John.

- We also know that when the positive side is heavier in the scale then we have profit.

- Crystal clear. - John agreed with me again.

- So what happens when your left side is the heavier side?

- You need that loan. - John started to laugh.

- Which is a temporary help right?

- Yes, of course but a huge and life saving help. - John tried to agree.

- Or a temporary help with a much higher obligation? - I challenged John's mind.

- Why? - he asked back. - Loan is a tool for survival.

- Loan is a tool if you have a rock hard strategy for a marketable product. - I started - However loan is a poison if you need it for survival.

- I did no understand it. - said John. - Draw please! - he smiled at me.

I smiled back and I started to draw him again.

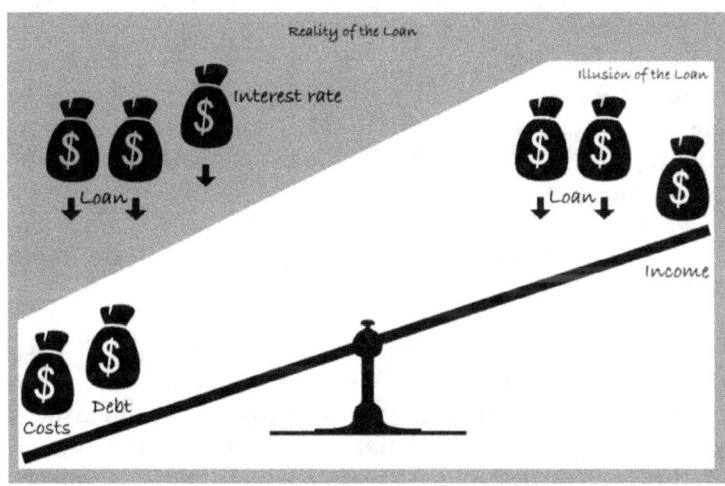

- When your company is in debt and you need money it means that you are not able to sell your products or services.

- Obviously. But maybe because of some other factor.

- It does not matter why. If you are not able to sell and you are not able to discover its reasons then you will not be able to find a solution for it. Therefore even if you receive a nice big amount of loan you still have no guarantee that you will be able to sell again, since you have not discovered the source of your non-performance.

- Please let me disagree. Loan supports you to survive difficult times.

- No, it is new incomes and profit that makes you survive difficult times.

- Those as well. - John laughed.

- Yes, but without them you are just digging your grave. You have to sell. Because when you get two bags of money, which at the end is actually three bags with the obligations, then you need to earn much more to pay back all the obligations. If you were not able to earn your costs and debt before the loan, then how could you earn your loan, its interest rate as well as your costs and debt?

I saw that John has no answer to this so I continued my line of thinking.

- A loan can be considered as a solution only in case you understand the way how you can sell. If you are unable to sell then it does not matter how much loan you take up, your performance indicators will go down at the end of the day. However if you can go back to the track by challenging the market and to sell again, then you do not need a loan. The problem is that banks are offering loans on golden plates as easy solutions, but it is far away from being an easy way.

- So no loan, right.

- Depends on... - I smiled back.

- On what?

- Whether you are able to sell or not. You can develop any kind of product if it stays on your stock. What will change? You have to learn to sell them. You have to learn to improve your income and to earn profit no matter what the economic climate is.

- By handling excuses, right?

Chapter 10
Excuses

- When you have a prospective client, which means that you know that he needs your product and possibly he has the funds for it as well, then everything depends on how you are able to handle the upcoming excuses.

- Is there always an excuse?

- What is your experience? - I could not stand not to laugh.

- Forget my question. - John laughed as well.

- Using an excuse is the natural game of the prospective client, which usually scares the sales guys. It has become a natural reaction that when we hear an excuse we immediately panic, start to give discounts or we believe that it is the end. Then a few months later we will hear that our prospective clients bought almost the same product from one of our competitors.

- I know this by heart. - John said.

- Then please start to handle them. Do not be scared, because it is all about practicing.

- And the result?

- The result of handling the excuses?

- Yes.

- Look, many prospective clients have a very clear intention to buy, however they are afraid of the commitment. Once they sign a contract the game has finished. Therefore they give excuses to gain more time, information or confidence before their final decision. If you are able to provide them the confidence they can still ask for more time. Therefore you need to control the process.

- Would you practice with me again? - John asked.

- Yes, sure. Drop me some excuses.

John seemed to be very excited and happy and I was sure that he has a much longer excuse list than before, however I was also sure that I am able to handle them.

- Let's get started - he smiled at me.

- Go on.

- I do not need this! - started John.

- If you would not need this we would not be sitting here - I replied him quickly.

- Nice. - said John - What if I repeat it? I really do not need this.

- I am pretty sure that your current system is working well John. I am also sure that it gives you the feeling of survival, but the only question is when would you like to start to develop and to grow. Because based on my own experience you can not survive for long on budget cuts and on solutions that do not support your activity. No business should live from its reserves. What I am offering here is a product and a tool to develop your business, to increase the number of your clients and to gain business and financial stability.

When I finished my sentence I watched John's reaction who was under shock.

- Wow. No words. - he started. - You turned that back on me nicely.

- Yes. Handling a prospective client is all about handling his excuses. You should never let a prospective client go away or think, because then you will have a great chance that he will buy from someone else.

- But you can not force him.

- No, but you can guide him.

- I should make some notes... - John said.

- It's not necessary because every case is different, such as every person you will meet and talk to. You have to feel this and also its limits.

- Limits? - he asked back.

- Yes, because sometimes you need to answer back in a very hard way and sometimes you need to handle the prospective client in a very gentle way. There are limitations.

- I understand. Shall we continue? - John asked.

I just gave him a sign with my hand that I am ready for the next round.

- How much is it?

- Much less than the result it brings you back in a very short time period.

- Hey-hey-hey. - John shouted. - You did not answer the question.

- Because I do not want to talk about the price. When you start to negotiate over the price you immediately go into the game of the prospective client. I never give them the chance to negotiate about the price. However I always answer in a different way.

- How many answers do you have?

- Endless. - I smiled at John.

- Okay. How much is it?

- I am giving you the tool, which you have been looking for since a long time. Something, which will improve your business. What do you think how much is it worth?

- How much is it?

- It is not important how much it is, what is important is that it brings you new clients.

- How much is it?

- It is not important how much it is, the importance is that it will close out your competitors.

- How much is it?

- It is not important how much it is, what is important is the reactions that it creates within the clients. You can spend less, but you can not be sure that you will deliver your brand message to the prospective clients.

- Okay, wait. - John said. - You are throwing back the same scheme.

- Yes, because you are repeating the same question. - I laughed at John.

- So you do not have any other idea? - he asked.

I started to feel that he is trying to challenge me in this but I really enjoyed it. I was ready for this challenge.

- So what is your next question? - I asked John.

- How much is it? - he smiled.

- Before I would say anything I have to tell you that it is a very expensive solution because this really works in real life. So should I stay or go?

- Could you tell me how much it is? - John challenged me further.

- Ten thousand. - I smiled at John.

- It is expensive!

- Yes it is. - I agreed with John - Not everyone can afford it, just as not every business survives.

- I do not need it!

- In order to develop your business, in order to gain more income you need this. Without this you will be continuously looking for another solution, which is waste of time. This solution is here and it helps you to gain results.

- But it is still expensive!

- Expensive are all those things that do not bring you result. In the past years I have had plenty dinners where the food was bad. Also I have been to movies that were boring. These things were very expensive, because I did not receive the expected result even if their cost were only a few hundred. However when something brings you the expected result then it can not be considered expensive.

- Yeah, but ten thousand? It is a fortune. - John smiled at me.

- If you buy something for one million, which brings you back twenty million in a very short time then was the one million expensive?

- No, but there are other cheaper solutions.

- Indeed. There are many cheaper solutions. And you can spend a real fortune trying all of them, however perhaps they will not bring you back the same result as this service I offer to you.

- Expensive...

- It is! - I replied quickly. - Because it is a premium product. It is not for everyone.

John started to be very exhausted, but he continued.

- It is still expensive.

- Look, my business is running well. I have made many new clients in the last few years, my company is running with profit. I do not need this deal with you. I am here to help you to grow and develop.

- Is it really working?

- If it would not be working I would never do this...

- But is it really working?

- I only promise something if I am hundred percent sure that it is working.

- So do you have any experience with this product?

- Yes. Look I have to tell you that in the beginning I had my doubts too. When I started to use this product I started to gain new clients and they started to spread the word regarding how good I am. Therefore I have gained additional new clients. This is why I trust this product.

- What is your guarantee? - John asked.

And here it is, this is my favorite question. People are always looking for guarantees. However in many cases you can not predict a future, which is specially true with business planning or consultations, which is my field of area. Of course you can work based on your life experiences and business knowledge or know-how but when you go into details they are always looking for the black spots to find a good reason not to buy. So I always drop this question back as hard as I can.

- My guarantee? - I asked back.

- Yes. - said John and I felt he is extremely satisfied because he thought he caught me. But he was far far away from the truth.

- People believe that sales and marketing is a logical process. If this would be true then we would not need anymore marketing and sales experts. It would be enough to put out a form into our website, and the prospective clients would spontaneously and immediately recognize it and they would just flow into our business. However it is not the way it works. This is why you need new points of view which is why I am here. Right?

John knew that he would be finished with this guarantees round if he would agree with my thoughts. Instead he immediately deflected the question and moved into another direction.

- We did not calculate with this amount in our budget. - John said.

- I am asking you to think about when do you want to start to really improve. When do you want new clients?

- Now, but it still does not fit the planned budget.

- If you want to make a deal next year it is perfectly fine for me, however I am not sure that this product will be available next year because of the serious amount of interest and its proven track record.

- Not in the budget. - John forced me further.

- No problem. Just a last remark, I am not able to book or hold this product for you and part of my obligation is to let you know that probably we will sell this product to another company in your field of business.

- Wow, that is harsh. - John replied.

- Which part?

- Selling it to my competitors? It sounds very rude.

- No, I never said that directly. - I smiled at John - I just pointed out that the product is good enough, so it will be sold.

- Let's go back! - John said - I am not sure that we can pay this amount this year.

- Look, the only way to work together if we can sign the contract this year and you are able to fulfill the payment.

- Nice try. - John said.

- Look, you just mentioned to me the key words.

- What key words? - John asked surprised.

- When people start to negotiate on the payment deadline you can be hundred percent sure that they desperately need your product. It is sure because their focus is not on the product anymore but on the "How can we pay this" issue.

I knew that John understood this. I was really curious how many times he has met with this situation without knowing that he was already in the finish line. Probably it was a lot but I did not want to ask him because I wanted to protect him from another negative impact, from some bad recognition. So I let him ask further questions.

- I have to talk this over with the headquarter of our branch.

- I know that you have multiple branches and of course a headquarter in New York. However we are in London now and we are looking to increase the performance indicators of the London office. As far as I know you are the responsible for these indicators and you need to show up the improvement. What would the New York headquarter say if you would not be able to grab the opportunity to improve?

- Yes, but I still have to talk this over with the headquarter.

- Of course. Just a last question what does the New York office want? Improvements and new clients, right? So do you think they would refuse an offer, which ensures all these?

John scratched the top of his head and then he looked into my eyes.

- You know Zsolt, if I would knew these answers before I would be much more relaxed now. - then he lifted his glass. - Cheers.

- Cheers - I replied back and we both enjoyed a bit of our tasty whisky.

- So, let's say I need to think about this.

- Okay, just try to feel the excuses and handle them easily.

- No, no - said John. - This is my next excuse. I need to think about this.

- Okay. So... - I tried to collect my thoughts. - If you would not need this we would not be sitting here.

- Ha-ha. I got you! You already said this.

- But this is good here as well, right? It is a universal one. - I smiled back.

- No other ideas?

- I am sorry but as I see you are looking for business improvements since many years. I am sure if you say yes to my offer you will not regret it.

- Not bad, but I have to compare it with other possible solutions.

- Of course, you are entitled to do it. However let me ask, since when are you looking for a solution like this? There are two things that are usually missing in a company: time and money. If you choose to look further you will loose time, which will result in an unnecessary delay concerning your improvement. I know from my experience that it can cause increased stress level. If we would sign a contract today then you could start to improve immediately, to gain more profit and not to mention that you could decrease your stress level.

- Probably you are right - John said, but I continued my thoughts immediately, giving no chance to John.

- Look, I am sure that you receive various business offers in a daily base specially in the field of your expertise. However as we both know it is the result that counts not the offer.

- Maybe it is true, but I have to think about this.

- John, I am in this business since sixteen years. Everyone who told me that they will think about my offer, could not come back to me with a better solution no matter how much time has passed by. As I mentioned to you money and time are always missing in a company. The only question is when is one ready to change all this.

Since I realized that John is giving me the same excuses over and over again, I decided to tell him some basic thoughts again. I was sure that he already forgot the main reason why we started this whole excuse topic.

- I see you enjoy this. - I said to John.

- Yes of course. Do you need a break?

- No, I just want to highlight something for you.

- I am listening.

- The thing is that we are only handling excuses in this way when we are sure that the prospective client has a serious interest in our product, therefore he needs it and he is also able to afford it.

- I know. - John said.

- Yes, and another very important thing is that no one has money to throw out of the window. So if you are sure about the intent but the prospective client has no money, you can still force him to change or reorganize his budget.

- Go it.

- So in real life probably you will never receive the same excuses over and over again.

- Okay, I understand your point. - John acknowledged me.

- Please do not misunderstand me, it is great if you are able to create a list of excuses. I suggest this to all my business partners. If you have a list of possible excuses attached with ways to handle them then you will be able to react faster. Many of my partners have weekly trainings as well for their sales people to practice this.

- Cool. I will have a list of excuses too. - John said in a very happy tone.

- I am glad.

- Zsolt, please one more topic.

- I am listening.

- What about the lawyers? - John asked.

- You mean by...? - I asked back.

- For example, the excuse of I have to check this with my lawyer.

- You just throw this back too.

- Okay, but how?

- Let's see... - I started - I completely agree with you because lawyers are the guardians of our businesses. But let's start with a letter of intent because this way we can start the improvement process immediately without loosing any delay.

- Another one? The last one I promise. - John said to me with a kind of prayer in his eyes.

- I have many clients in various business sectors. I have worked for IBM, SWAROVSKI, Carrefour, Alstom Power and many other big corporate giants, and I never experienced any problem with our contracts. Of course we can let the lawyers double-check it, however in the meantime let's start with a letter of intent.

- So do you allow the lawyer?

- Look, the one thing that is important is that you can not attack your prospective client. However you can give him more information. Lawyer issue is always a tricky part of the business because a legal advisor is always busy, therefore it takes much more time and you will have no chance to influence him and let the lawyer know why your product is ideal for his client.

- Exactly.

- So you can ensure them the possibility to check everything with the lawyer but before you should get a letter of intent.

- Why? - John asked curiously.

- Because if you have a letter of intent then you have a deal. My experience is that without a letter of intent you can lose your business when it gets to the lawyer because he can always find a small thing, which can destroy your chances. However if you have an intent then the lawyers will be in a position where they need to correct only the mistakes in the following contract instead of refusing the whole co-operation. When they acknowledge that their client needs you then they will help the process. This is why you have to have a letter of intent before the lawyer receives anything.

- Last question. - John said.

- Go on, I am listening.

- What if they really do not have money?

This was the point where we both knew that this is a completely new story.

Chapter 11
It is not enough

- Here is one of the basic rule my friend. If you are sure that your prospective client has no funds to afford your solution or product then you should not waste your time with him.

- But maybe later, maybe next year. - John said.

Oh, gosh. It was something that I did not expect from John. It was so naive, almost a rookie entrepreneur mistake.

- When you are planning your product development you are analyzing the past and present and you are making plans for the future. However when you are thinking only about your own business survival then you have no time for the future. If you are going this year only to clients who can not buy your product now, you are risking to go bankrupt even before they will have funds to sign anything with you.

- So what is your opinion?

- My opinion for what? - I looked at John with surprise.

- How can you select people who have real money?

- This is where you can utilize your marketing team.

- But it is sales. - John said.

- Not really. Many people make the mistake that they use the same person for marketing, sales and PR however those are three very different fields with completely different needs. The PR has the responsibility to spread the message about your company and its results. The marketing has the responsibility to find out where the prospective clients are and it is also a marketing task to bring them to the door of your company. The marketing ensures all the basic information to the prospective clients and your marketing team should have to decide whether the client is prospective or not.

- So what does the sales do? - John asked.

- The sales creates the personal contact and they are the ones who close the deal. The sales is working from a well selected list, therefore they can focus on the sales closing and income.

- Got it. - John acknowledged it.

The one thing that I was sure about tonight was that John will have a very hard next week. I knew that he will think about all the issues he heard and he will manage some changes in his company.

- But you know John to achieve good sales closings and to handle the excuses effectively you have to know many other things, such as the industry of your target group, the requested data for the decision, the client type, etc... Not to mention that there are no magic pills.

- Magic pills? - John asked with a surprise.

- Yeah, magic pills. You know there are big differences between expensive and effective marketing. - I started to expand my thoughts - Many companies are spending incredible amounts for various marketing campaigns, advertisements and they spend money without any limits on these. They are using the "pure power rule", which philosophy means that if you see everywhere their advertisement then probably you will be hypnotized to buy their product sooner or later. However many of these campaigns are unable to reach the planned results since standard marketing does not work anymore.

- I know these type of people. - John winked.

- With an effective and well developed marketing strategy you can reach impressive results without spending a fortune on advertisements, which are targeting the big mass. A good marketing campaign is able to reach your well defined target group and is able to make them react. However unlike many great "marketing courses" or "ready made packages" there is no magic pill. There is a lot of hard work, which can produce results based on best practices, that are moved by real experiences.

- Always the hard work...

- And the experience, life experience, which gives us more choices and possibilities to challenge situations. However you should not forget that there are different business sectors and some of them have very special rules.

- Not in my field.

- Then there are the different type of decision makers, therefore different type of clients.

- What do you mean?

- For example the individual woman, the family man, the professional buyers and the weak ones. There are many personal types and you can not handle all of them in the same way. You have to understand the differences and the physical reactions.

- I believe that we will have no time to talk them over, right? - John asked.

- Not tonight my friend, not tonight.

NO EXCUSE! in business
- written by Zsolt Szemerszky -

As I said this to John I saw that he became a little bit sad and disappointed. He was so keen to get to know these client types but we had no time for this. However I decided to give him some extra information.

- Look let's see some basic issues that you really need to know before you send out a sales guy.

- Really? That's great. Thank you Zsolt.

- The very basic topics, which will give you a basic understanding regarding the needs of the client are:

➡ What does he want?

➡ What could the best solution be for him?

➡ What are his aims and goals with it?

➡ What are the things which worry him?

➡ Do you have references in a similar industry, or with similar products?

- Got it.

- These are the very basic things that you should know beforehand. But to achieve real positive decisions you need to know much more. My companies always put high priority on the personal data, such as:

➡ client name

➡ contact (address, telephone, fax, email, website, facebook, twitter, linkedIn, etc...)

➡ family status, kids

➡ birthdays and anniversaries

➡ known friends - which is very important because they are able to influence him

➡ hobbies vs. things he does not like

- Yes, but to know information like these you need to meet with him.

- Indeed. This is why you are starting with the needs, goals and worries because it gives you a basic insight, all the additional information will develop with time. If you categorize him as a prospective client then you need to start to collect many information about him. It will be very useful in the future as well.

- Do you collect company information as well?

- Of course! - I replied promptly.

- Such as?

- Let's see...

➡ company

➡ contact (address, telephone, fax, email, website, facebook page, twitter, etc...)

➡ ownership structure

➡ decision makers

➡ year of foundation

➡ activities

➡ products, distributors and suppliers

➡ plans and objectives

➡ difficulties

➡ number of employees

➡ income vs. profit before tax

➡ trends (employees, income, clients)

- So you are the FBI. - John laughed.

- Not really, but it is always good to take some notes about your partners. This can help you in the future.

For example you make a note of "Company A" which will not buy from you at the end. However a few months later you will meet with "Company B" and you will realize that the owner's best friend is the owner of "Company A". Therefore you can prepare a strategy because you learnt from the first one and you already know his opinion and reactions. You can use it as a tool or as a weapon.

- Go it. - John acknowledged everything I told him during the past two hours.

- It is very important to know what you are dealing with when you are entering the door. When I started my business I had many bad experiences with big companies. Of course it was my mistake because I did not understand the rules.

- What rules?

- The rule of fear.

- What? - John looked at me extremely surprised.

- Yes. You know big corporations usually like small companies. Small companies usually have owners with an excellent mind. Probably they had a great and innovative idea and this is why they were motivated to start their own company. Therefore they are innovators and probably they know something, which can make difference in the field of their business. This is what makes them very valuable in the eyes of the big corporates.

- So where is the problem?

- The problem is that the big ones will never buy from them.

- Why?

- Let me tell you just a few reasons:

➡ They can do it from their own resources.

➡ They can present the idea as their own to the existing suppliers.

➡ They can contract with another big company.

- I do not understand this? Why would they contract with another company instead of the source.

- Because it is another game, which leads to another excuse. The excuse of fear. Let me explain it to you in depth. Decision makers are usually scared to make a bad decision, which can risk their position. Therefore they are also afraid to explain to their management board why they chose a young company instead of a well established old one. As you know the saying: "Nobody was ever fired by choosing IBM."

- What a bullshit.

- No, it is a safe game. But they still need the innovative ideas.

- So they are just playing with the idea makers?

- Usually yes. They give them the carrot that their product is very interesting and they are forcing the small ones to ensure as much information as it is possible. So at the end of the day they do not really need the idea owner anymore.

- But somebody has to develop it.

- The big corporation has many resources for this. The key is not this but how you handle this.

- Can you handle this?

- Of course. See this as a big excuse.

- I can not see it, sorry.

- But you have to. Okay. Where is the excuse? Why are they not ready to contract with the small innovator?

- Because of the fear of small? - John answered.

- Exactly! - I applaud for him. - So you have to handle this. For example you can involve a bigger contractor who gives his name for the final contract.

- Does this work?

- When I started my IT company very long time ago we lost many of the prospective big clients. However I realized its source and I became an IBM Business Partner. After this we went to the big companies in IBM colours, under IBM hats. IBM always sent one or two guys to support us and we always arrived as a working team to the clients. The client was extremely satisfied to sign a contract with a trusted corporate giant and we were satisfied too because finally we got the orders.

- But IBM took a big portion right?

- Yes. But having a share from the pie is always better than having nothing. And this was very relative because do not forget that what originally cost hundred thousand we sold now for two hundred because price did not really matter at this point. Bigger contractor bigger respect. Therefore we did not have to lose money on the deals.

- Smart. - John liked it.

This was the point when our dessert finally arrived. I was so happy for it because I had no more place on my tea-cloth and I really wanted to enjoy the rest of the dinner. Luckily John was in the same opinion as well, or maybe he just recognized that I am not here to consult him. However I was really happy to give him some new directions and ideas. He was always a good audience because he not just listen to me but made some notes too. I knew that he is an experimenting type of guy so I was sure that he will implement many thoughts I gave him into his business, and this felt good.

We also agreed that we will meet next week for two-three days and we will talk over these issues more in detail, and I will create him a business strategy as well as a training course for his sales team regarding handling excuses.

John was on the track to renew and improve his business. He was on the road of profit growing. He just needed an outside view.

After the dessert we finally reached the cigar time, which was always the highlight of the day for me. I asked for another Chivas Regal and we moved out to the terrace to light our big fat Cuban ambassadors. It was a very delightful feeling to blow that little smoke cloud into the dark sky.

Chapter 12
The mask of success

At some point of my relaxation covered by the sweet and crispy smoke clouds I heard John's voice again.

- So this is like success, right?

- What do you mean?

- To live in Monte-Carlo and to enjoy life. Enjoy a nice dinner, smoke a nice cigar. This is how you imagined your life, right? - asked John.

- Not really. You know success has its prize and its price as well. During so many years I painted success in a very different way.

- What do you mean?

- When I received the National Quality Prize in 2006 I was very proud of myself. I felt that people really appreciate what I am doing for them. It felt really great. However I realized that from that point on I needed to give them much more. I had to prove that my creativity did not end there and that I was able to bring much more innovation. So I did it.

- So it motivated you to improve. Where is the trap?

- The trap came in 2008 when I became the Entrepreneur of the Year in my field.

- What a big trap... Shame on the committee. - John joked.

- You know when you are gaining success you will start to collect envious people around you.

- Who cares? It is bad for them.

- Yes, but no. - I said to John - You know Sir Winston Churchill said that "You have enemies? Good. That means you've stood up for something, something in your life.". And I agree with Mr. Churchill, however I received numberless critics, envious mails, blaming and accusations in my life from people who are unsuccessful in their life and in their own fields of area. It was very hard to digest this in the beginning, then I realized this is how it works. It is very funny and also very interesting but for a long time I did not know that there is a scientific explanation and an official name for this behavior, called Schadenfreude.

- Do not give a crap about them. - John tried to calm me down.

- You know first I did not. Then I started to see how these people are impersonating me, creating messages in my name, blogs, facebook accounts, etc. I became really sad. However my very close friend Dodo Newman helped me out from this period and she lightened me up. I realized that all successful people have enemies. I came back to the reality of Mr. Churchill and I started to understand why celebrities are hiding and drinking. I realized that success involves the balance of nature, so when you increase the good in your life you will also attract more the negative effect as well. This is the balance of life. However it is up to you how much negative effect you allow into your life.

- Do you remember the facebook movie? - asked John.
- You can not have hundred million fans without having some enemies... Or something like that.

- I know John. I know it. - I smiled at him. - I am in a way over this. However I would like to see others really understand things. For example I do not care if someone writes something about me, specially not until it does not appear in the New York Times. The source, which is credibility and proven results are the two most important things in my life.

- Let's drink to them.

- To the results - I lifted up my glass.

- So does this really bug you? - John asked.

- No I just wanted to reflect to your thought and I wanted to let you know that you are doing good my friend! Because we are bears on the flower field!

- What? Bears on the flower field? What the hell are you talking about? Too much drink?

- When I was younger I met with a very wise guy in a conference. He mentioned to me that people get stuck in small details and they forget the real results.

- Agreed. - John acknowledged it.

- He also told me a short story about the bear who one day walks around a flower field. Suddenly the bear sees a big mug of honey on the other side of the field. Honey reflects the possibility of our aim.

- I am not stupid. - John smiled.

- So the bear moves by instinct, which means he runs across the field towards the mug of honey. The only thing that he has in mind is that he really wants the honey on the other side of the field. However when he finally gets it, achieves it he realizes that during the crossing he stamped on some flowers. He moved by instinct and he chose the shortest way towards his aim, the honey without taking the long way to get around the field. Did he do the wrong thing?

- If he leaves the flowers yes.

- Thank you for the IF. Because it is all about the intent. So when the bear realized what he did on the road towards his aim he went back to the field and he helped the flowers, which he stamped on before and he also planted some new flowers. So he corrected and improved his environment.

- Good bear! - John laughed while he lifted his glass.

- Inventors and visionaries are experimenting something new, they are challenging the existing rules so they will always make mistakes. But the intent is what really counts and the result at the end of the day.

- I agree with you little bear.

- Come on John! I am telling this to you so you understand that if you are able to master all the excuses you will be able to create your own success. However no matter what, do not let people take away the results you gain. Be proud of them and specially be proud because you have tried to change something in your situation.

- I know it. I am proud already. - said John.

Chapter 13
It is time to say goodbye

As the night passed by we realized that we finished smoking our cigars and our glasses were empty. It was time to say goodbye. We fixed our next meeting and I also promised John that I will send him a copy of my new book titled "Mountain of Result".

On the way out John turned to me:

- Zsolt you are a good friend of mine. Thank you for this. - he said.

- It is my pleasure to know you.

- Do you consider me as a friend? - John asked with a little hesitation in his voice.

I could not stand not to quote a thought from my favorite TV series "Boston Legal".

- "People walk around today calling everyone their best friend. The term doesn't have any real meaning anymore. Mere acquaintances are lavished with hugs and kisses upon a second or at most third meeting, birthday cards get passed around offices so everybody can scribble a snippet of sentimentality for a colleague they barely met, and everyone just loves everyone. As a result when you tell somebody you love them today, it isn't much heard." But you are my friend John and I really appreciate this friendship. - I said to him.

John shook my hand and walked away with new hopes and high satisfaction.

NO EXCUSE! in business
- *written by Zsolt Szemerszky* -

Liability disclaimer

This book/e-book is not a substitute for independent professionals, investment or legal advice. Present book serves as the writer's interpretation of his personal business views, without specific advice on any personal or corporate requirements. Use of any information from this book or any other book or web site referred to is for general information only and does not represent advice either expressed or implied. You are encouraged to seek professional, legal or investment advice.

Accordingly, the author, his publishers and affiliates disclaim that the information provided should not be treated as advice. Furthermore, it is a strict condition of the that any individual reading the book recognizes and accepts unreservedly that all information, analyses, projections, forecasts, expectations, or outcomes relating to past, present, or future financial markets performance, economic activity, or investment or trading instruments, are provided exclusively for academic purposes and that such information must not in any way be construed as general or personal advice to invest or trade in any financial market or security.

The author or publishers shall not be held liable for any losses incurred by anyone who follows or acts on the opinions, views, or forecasts expressed in any form in this e-book, on any other websites or from individuals connected by hyperlink to or from this website. Anyone reading this book is solely responsible for their interpretation of its contents and for their own decisions and actions. The foregoing applies also to correspondence (including private emails), to posts on other websites (including internet message boards and public discussion forums), and to articles published in other mass media.